Diesels Over The Roof of England

By
Michael S. Welch

First Published 2003

ISBN 0 946184 81 X

Published By
Waterfront

A Division of Kingfisher Productions

The Dalesmade Centre, Watershed Mill, Settle,

North Yorkshire BD24 9LR

Printed by The Amadeus Press, Cleckheaton, West Yorkshire

Above: The early evening shadows are just starting to encroach in the foreground as Class 40 No. 40 069 passes Baron Wood with the 3.37pm Carlisle to Leeds train on 23rd October 1982. The magnificent autumn colours provide a splendid setting. No. 40 069 emerged from Vulcan Foundry in April 1960 and lasted in service for a further eleven months after this picture was taken.
Bob Leslie

Front cover: In this splendidly evocative study, BR/Sulzer 1Co-Co1 Type 4 No. D35, in charge of the 10.25am Leeds to Glasgow train, emerges from the confines of Blea Moor tunnel into Dentdale on a July day in 1967. Note that the locomotive is in very presentable external condition. The signal post adjacent to the third coach of the train was formerly Dent Head's down distant, and was a vintage MR lower quadrant signal on a square post. No. D35 became No. 45 117 under the TOPS renumbering scheme, and lasted in service until May 1986. It was scrapped at Vic Berry's Leicester yard in January 1987. *J. Spencer Gilks*

Back cover: When the passenger train service over the S&C line was increased in the mid-1980s to cater for expanding traffic this move, perhaps, marked a turning point in the line's fortunes. This development also had the side effect, no doubt welcomed by railway photographers, that services ran for a longer period during the day, thus providing greater photographic possibilities. In the early 1980s the first train left Carlisle for Leeds at the remarkably late time of 10.40am, but in the May 1987 timetable recast a new, early morning departure from Carlisle was introduced. This view shows the 6.30am *ex*-Carlisle, hauled by Class 47 No. 47 595 *Confederation of British Industry*, approaching Garsdale in brilliant early morning light in July 1988. *Author*

Title page: The up 'Royal Scot' from Glasgow to London passes Dent station behind Brush Type 4 No. D1849 in October 1966. Note the colourful composition of the train, which is led by the locomotive in two-tone green livery while, in total contrast, the vehicle formed immediately behind the engine is a Mk.2 brake first corridor coach in the (then) relatively new blue and grey colours. The remaining coaches in the shot are Mk.1s in traditional maroon livery. Quite an assortment of colours, which help brighten up the scene on, what appears to have been, a dull day.
Neville Simms

Introduction

The Settle & Carlisle line's spectacular, wild landscape and remarkable history ensured its special place in the affections of countless railway enthusiasts. Despite this, in steam days it was not widely photographed, and this is also true of much of the diesel era. Most photographers visiting the area often preferred the West Coast Main Line (WCML) which offered a better frequency and variety. The first appearance of diesel traction on the S&C line was probably way back in the mid-1950s when the prototype 'Deltic' worked test trains over the route, one such occasion being 28th August 1956 when this machine was recorded leaving Appleby on a southbound working. The first regular workings are understood to have been those of Metrovick Co-Bo locomotives on the 'Condor' overnight freight from London to Glasgow but, for obvious reasons, the author has been unable to trace any pictures! In June 1961 BR/Sulzer 2,500hp Type 4s, commonly known as 'Peaks', took over haulage of most of the line's through passenger workings and this event heralded the class's long association with the route.

During the 1960s, when diesel locomotives in green livery were an everyday sight, most enthusiasts who visited the line were chasing steam traction and many shunned diesels, but despite this some diesel shots were taken during that distinctive period. The S&C line probably reached the height of its popularity with diesel photographers in the early 1980s. This was brought about by the combination of two factors, firstly the dreadful news of the possibility of closure was publicised for the first time and, secondly, the route was still a regular stamping

Above: Pictured in glorious evening lighting conditions, the last surviving English Electric 2,000hp Type 4 in BR service, No. D200, nears Settle with a return Leeds to Carlisle special on 8th March 1986. *Author*

ground for many 1960s vintage diesel types which were steadily being phased out. Perhaps the most tangible evidence of the threat facing the line became apparent during this period when, in May 1982, the route's long distance passenger workings were re-routed via the West Coast Main Line, leaving the S&C with only a purely local Leeds to Carlisle service (and vice versa) consisting of only two trains per day. A number of freight workings remained, but these were being steadily diverted onto other routes and the remaining through freights were withdrawn altogether in May 1983. Some freight and ballast traffic existed, however, at each end of the line, but there was none between Ribblehead and Appleby, where there were barely sufficient trains to keeping the rails shiny! Engineering work on the WCML sometimes brought an upsurge of diverted passenger traffic to the S&C line at week-ends, and on one famous occasion Class 40 No. 40 152 appeared at the head of the up 'Royal Scot', much to the surprise and pleasure of many lineside observers.

Despite the ruthless policy of removing traffic from the line in order to strengthen the case for closure, a remarkable selection of diesel types could still be seen on the S&C route ranging from Class 25s to Class 47s. The Class 40s, in particular, were extremely popular with diesel haulage enthusiasts and 'Whistler'- hauled trains were noticeably well filled whenever they appeared. The enthusiasts who suddenly turned up whenever a Class 40 was rostered clearly had impeccable sources of information. Apart from No. D200 (40 122), the Class 40s sadly disappeared at the end of 1984, when the type was withdrawn *en masse*. During 1985 a novel development was the diagramming of the Hull to Carlisle train (and return) for a pair of Class 31s. The need for two of these machines reflected the weight of passenger trains, which had increased steadily from the all-time low reached in 1982 when four coaches often sufficed for the small number of travellers. The final appearance of a 'Peak' in ordinary service on the S&C was reportedly on 27th May 1987 when No. 45 033 worked on a northbound passenger train. This ended the class's links with the line which lasted 26 years. The elimination of the older diesel types, and introduction of the rather characterless 'Sprinters' on passenger trains in the early 1990s robbed the S&C of much of its interest, though this has been balanced to some extent by the re-introduction of freight traffic.

I have had the privilege of compiling two previous books on the S&C line, both devoted to the BR steam era, and this is my first album about diesels over the route. It has been immensely enjoyable selecting and captioning the pictures, and I am grateful to the many talented photographers who have so generously made their irreplaceable transparencies available for a wider audience to enjoy. Thanks are also due to Chris Evans, who kindly perused the manuscript and suggested many worthwhile improvements. Finally, I must not forget Roger Hardingham, my publisher, without whom this book would never have seen the light of day.

M.S.Welch, Burgess Hill, West Sussex, January 2003

Left: Photographed against the stunning background of Dentdale and the distant fells, an unidentified Class 25 crosses Dent Head viaduct with the morning Carlisle to Leeds train in September 1983. *Author*

HELLIFIELD TO RIBBLEHEAD

Top right: Class 24 Type 2 Bo-Bo No. 5113 is pictured at Hellifield on 19th September 1971 while powering a short train formed of a Civil Engineer's Department crane. The train is facing southwards and, most strangely, standing on the down line, so presumably it was working under a track possession during engineering operations. Hellifield station only serves a small village, but in times gone by it was a major junction and most of the Midlands Railway's (MR) Anglo-Scottish expresses stopped there. Hellifield's expansion as a railway centre started in earnest in 1880 when the Lancashire & Yorkshire Railway (L&YR) opened its route from Blackburn and a new, larger station was built to handle the Lancashire traffic. During the period prior to the First World War the MR was at the zenith of its powers, and ran six day-time and four night-time services to Scotland daily, and corresponding return trains. Through carriages were also provided from Manchester and Liverpool, and Hellifield was dealing with an incredible ninety trains a day! After that period its importance declined and it lost its purpose as a passenger junction when the Blackburn line trains were withdrawn in September 1962. By the date of this picture Hellifield had fallen on really hard times, as evidenced here by the rather neglected state of the buildings. The station has listed building status, however, and has been restored, but the Class 24 did not merit such special treatment and met its end at Doncaster Works in 1977. *Peter Fitton*

Bottom right: Class 40 No. 40 199 takes an afternoon freight past Settle Junction some time during the autumn of 1979. Part of Settle Junction signal box can just be identified above the bushes on the right. The single-lead junction layout seen here was installed following a serious accident on 2nd May 1979 when 41 vehicles of the 7.50pm (previous day) St. Blazey to Carlisle freight train, hauled by No. 40 023, were derailed causing extensive track damage. This incident occurred at a particularly unfortunate time because the East Coast Main Line was blocked north of Newcastle due to a rockfall in Penmanshiel tunnel, and the S&C was being used as a diversionary route for freight traffic. Settle Junction was also the site of one of the MR's shortest-lived stations, this being open for only a year from November 1876. *John Whiteley*

Photographed on a lovely September evening in 1988, a Class 47-hauled Carlisle to Leeds train approaches Settle Junction on the final stage of its long descent from Blea Moor. Apart from the vehicle marshalled immediately behind the locomotive, the train appears to be composed solely of BR Standard Mk. 1 coaches, which were being rapidly replaced by 'Sprinter' units on other routes at this time. Presumably, the S&C line, which was still under the threat of closure, was not regarded as a top priority for 'modernisation', and anyway many passengers preferred the more spacious Mk.1 carriages, which, unlike the 'Sprinters' had a window at every corner seat! The tracks of the line to Carnforth are in the foreground, while the top of Pen-y-Ghent is visible above the trees on the right.

Jim Winkley

A damp and dismal day at Settle! The morning Skipton to Carlisle local train collects a small contingent of passengers at the station on 22nd April 1970. Note the neatly kept flower beds and substantially-built station buildings with their decorative bargeboards. At this time the premises were still gas-lit, the lamp standards being painted in the London Midland Region's (LMR) 'standard' colours. Despite the gloom, the signal box and goods shed are just visible in the background. In the summer 1969 timetable the stopping train service from Skipton to Carlisle consisted of two return workings each weekday, these being supplemented by a morning Appleby to Carlisle train and its corresponding evening return train. There was also an early morning working from Garsdale to Leeds, but no return service was advertised. Note the d.m.u.'s window bars, which were fitted to Carlisle-based units for working the line from there to Barrow via Whitehaven, which has restricted clearances.   *Peter Fitton*

For a short period in the mid-1980s the morning Leeds to Carlisle train started from Hull and the corresponding return working ran through to Hull in the evening. This was hardly a traditional route for S&C trains, but at least it widened the potential market for these services. It is likely that this alteration was made for BR's operating convenience: perhaps the coaches were based at Hull! In this shot Class 47 No. 47 459, working the 7.38am Hull to Carlisle train, catches the morning sunshine as it slowly accelerates up the 1 in 100 gradient after leaving Settle on 8th March 1986. The coming of the railway changed the face of this small market town. The line is carried high above the town on two separate viaducts: Marshfield viaduct is just beyond the station while Settle (or Church) viaduct crosses the A65 road. Beyond the latter the railway was built on a huge embankment for which a million cubic yards of earth were reportedly used.

Author

A diverted West Coast Main Line express, hauled by an unidentified English Electric Type 4 Co-Co locomotive (later Class 50), threads the Stainforth Gorge on a Sunday in July 1971. The train is crossing the 58 yards-long Sheriff Brow viaduct that carries the railway across the foaming waters of the river Ribble. It is a skew bridge with massive wing retaining walls, and is one of three railway bridges across the river between Settle and Horton-in-Ribblesdale. These Type 4s were fairly regular visitors to the S&C line, on services diverted from the Shap route due to engineering works, from their introduction in late 1967 until 1974, when the Crewe to Glasgow line was electrified. The locomotives were then transferred *en masse* to the Western Region.

Jim Winkley

In order to provide a straight alignment for the railway, north of Sheriff Brow viaduct the line occupies the course of the river Ribble, which had to be diverted at this point. A second crossing of the river was necessary only a few hundred yards north of Sheriff Brow, and in this illustration BR/Sulzer Class 46 No. 46 002 is depicted speeding above the river with a Nottingham to Glasgow express on 12th April 1980. This structure is sometimes known as Little viaduct. Note the marked difference in the height above the river between these two bridges, which are less than a quarter of a mile apart.

Peter Fitton

The 11.50am Glasgow Central to Nottingham train, powered by Class 45 1Co-Co1 No. 45 002, crosses the river Ribble at Helwith Bridge on 1st May 1982. A few weeks later this Anglo-Scottish service, which consisted of three weekday trains each way, was diverted to run via Preston, thus heralding the run-down of the S&C line. These trains, which were the last surviving remnant of the MR's traditional Anglo-Scottish services, had replaced the famous 'Thames-Clyde Express', and other St. Pancras to Glasgow trains, in the mid-1970s. On the S&C line, the Glasgow to Nottingham trains were covered by a meagre service of two trains in each direction on weekdays, between Leeds and Carlisle only.

John Whiteley

In this really vintage colour picture, a rake of three 2-car Derby Lightweight d.m.u.s is shown entering Horton-in-Ribblesdale station on Sunday 5th July 1959. At that time the S&C line was still almost a totally steam-worked line (happy days!) and the appearance of this train of diesel units was, therefore, most unusual. Diesels were not introduced on the 'Thames-Clyde Express', for example, until two years later. The photographer describes the train as a 'Pennine diesel going north', which tends to suggest that this was a special Sunday excursion for hikers, and this is borne-out by the train reporting number in the cab window. Judging by the presence of window bars on the doors, it is likely that the train was returning to Carlisle as these were generally fitted to Carlisle-based units. Note the rather ridiculous 'speed whiskers' which were applied to the cab ends of these units until yellow warning panels came into vogue. Local people who may have been impressed by these units had only seven years to wait until they replaced steam on the S&C's local services!

Neil Thexton

Class 47 Co-Co No. 47 547 descends from Selside towards Horton-in-Ribblesdale with the 10.40am Carlisle to Leeds train on 8th March 1986. The five Mk.1 coaches forming the train seem to be reasonably well filled for the time of year, and the rake appears to include a stray ScotRail vehicle. The locomotive was built at Crewe Works in January 1965 as No. D1642 and was initially allocated to Newport (Ebbw Junction) shed in South Wales. It became No. 47 058 under the TOPS re-numbering scheme in September 1974 and was later fitted with electric train heating equipment, when it became No. 47 547. This was a memorable day of glorious, continuous sunshine on which Class 5MT No. 5305 hauled a Leeds to Carlisle special, which later returned behind No. D200, so photographers were well rewarded. The thick cable in the foreground was the subject of many caustic remarks by lineside photographers, but a fortunate 'sag' at this location enabled a clear view of the locomotive to be obtained. *Author*

A Carlisle to Leeds d.m.u. is seen amidst the bleak, inhospitable moorland, which typifies Upper Ribblesdale. The brooding presence of Pen-y-Ghent dominates this scene, which was photographed on 25th March 1989. The wide-open spaces of this area are in marked contrast to the narrow Stainforth Gorge, just a few miles up the line. The course of the river Ribble is visible above the last coach of the train.

Jim Winkley

A southbound freight, headed by Class 47 No. 47 221, passes a row of MR cottages between Ribblehead and Selside on a gloriously clear summer's day in 1980. The row of six terrace houses was built on the site of Salt Lake City, a shanty town used by navvies employed on construction work for the S&C line back in the 1870s. These sturdily-built houses were similar in design to those being constructed in northern industrial towns at the time, rather than the moorland farm cottages, which are dotted about this area. This row of houses is still known as 'Salt Lake City' today, thus maintaining a link with the past. Other navvy encampments were also given colourful names, such as Sebastopol, Jericho and Belgravia. *Les Nixon*

Its downhill all the way (at least as far as Settle Junction!) for this pair of English Electric Type 4 Co-Co locomotives, as they descend from Ribblehead towards Horton-in-Ribblesdale with a diverted West Coast express in May 1973. The leading locomotive is No. 428 and the train is formed almost entirely of early Mk.2 non air-conditioned coaching stock. From Hellifield the train would have been routed via the (then) freight-only line to Blackburn and along the East Lancashire line probably to Preston, where it would have reversed. If the train had not been booked to stop at Preston it would have traversed a curve at Farington, providing a direct run to Crewe and the south.

A.E.R. Cope

The unmistakable setting of Ribblehead station with Whernside, one of the three peaks of this area, forming the backdrop. The train is the 11.55am Hellifield to Carlisle 'all-stations', formed of a Derby Lightweight d.m.u. and this shot was taken on 21st September 1966. This exposed spot is noted for its strong winds and notoriously high rainfall, and many years ago Ribblehead station's remarkable climatic conditions were given official recognition when it became an Air Ministry weather station. Note what appears to be an anemometer on the top of the pole on the right. In order to keep out the harsh weather the walls of the stationmaster's cottage at Ribblehead were tile-hung to provide extra protection. Unfortunately the original down platform here was removed to facilitate construction of a stone terminal, so an identical picture cannot be repeated today. A new platform has, however, recently been erected.

Peter Fitton

17

RIBBLEHEAD TO GARSDALE

During the early 1980s, the LMR pursued a relentless policy of diverting traffic away from the S&C line in an attempt to prove that the route was of negligible traffic value and surplus to operating requirements. May 1982, as previously mentioned, saw the re-routing of the Nottingham to Glasgow expresses and, exactly a year later, the last remaining through freights ran. These were the 3.45am and 3.20pm Healey Mills to Carlisle and 1.10pm Carlisle to Healey Mills plus the 10.30am Mossend to Healey Mills. In addition to these trains there were regular workings from Carlisle to Warcop army depot, and to Ribblehead stone terminal, which were unaffected by these changes. On the morning of 13th May 1983, the last day of through freight operations, the penultimate booked down train passed through Dentdale in appropriately gloomy weather conditions following a deluge, headed by Class 40 No. 40 085. But one of the fascinations of the S&C line is the ever-changing weather, and by the time No. 40 085 reappeared with the early afternoon train from Carlisle the day had been transformed: it was pleasantly warm and mostly sunny. Here, No. 40 085 has just come off Ribblehead viaduct, which is partiallly visible, and continues the long descent down the 'Long Drag' towards Settle. *Author*

Many railway photographers have probably complained about the S&C line's notoriously unpredictable weather patterns. In the winter, bitter cold and howling winds are often experienced, while the summer months frequently produce mist and haze, which mask the route's scenic delights, as evidenced here by this picture taken at Ribblehead in July 1979. A distant outline of Ingleborough is just visible through the mist. The train in view is a northbound freight powered by Class 40 No. 40 122, which at that time was a completely anonymous machine, just one of many of these locomotives which were a daily sight on the S&C line on unbraked freight trains, usually formed of short wheelbase vehicles. The number of unbraked freight workings over the S&C line had increased markedly following the resignalling and removal of catch points from the West Coast Main Line in the mid-1970s. No. 40 122, was, of course, formerly D200 and the first of its class to be built, in 1958.

Author

In contrast to the weather conditions seen in the previous illustration, Class 47 No. 47 377 is depicted approaching Blea Moor in charge of a northbound freight in August 1982. It had been a wet morning, but the clouds rolled away to produce a beautifully bright, clear afternoon and evening, thus enabling a variety of workings to be photographed in almost perfect conditions. In addition to the train seen here, there was Class 46 No. 46 046 on a southbound freight and a Class 31 on the afternoon Carlisle to Leeds passenger train, while Class 25s powered both the Leeds to Carlisle passenger train and a stone working from Ribblehead quarry. The latter ran up to Blea Moor to run round, so could be photographed twice. What more could a lineside photographer wish for, a clean 'Black Five' slogging uphill on a heavy freight, perhaps? *Author*

Top right: Confrontation at Blea Moor! An adventurous sheep almost comes to a premature end at Blea Moor on 10th September 1983, and causes considerable amusement to the hoards of Class 40 haulage fanatics on board the train. Sheep in this part of the world roam freely, and their antics have caused considerable trouble for the railway authorities, particularly since some of the lineside dry stone walls fell into disrepair. This prompted BR to construct an extra wire fence in places to repel the animals. The locomotive which is the subject of the enthusiasts' adoration is No. 40 013 (formerly *Andania*), which was one of the earliest examples to be built and lasted until the end of the class (apart from No. 40 122) in January 1985. On the left is Blea Moor signal box, one of the most isolated in Great Britain, which is accessible only on foot across a moorland path from the nearest road located over a mile away. In steam days enginemen were always thankful when the signal box came into view: it indicated that the summit of the climb from Settle Junction, which is located just inside Blea Moor tunnel, was only a mile away. The outermost tracks are loop lines, which were installed as a wartime measure in December 1941.   *Peter Fitton*

Bottom right: A magazine reader, whose letter about diesel locomotive design was published back in the 1960s, stated unflatteringly that the average BR express was headed by 'a shapeless lump of filth'. Maybe this was a slight exaggeration but, who knows, perhaps 'Peak' No. D34 sparked his criticism. This locomotive was photographed during the summer of 1967 leaving Blea Moor tunnel with the up 'Waverley' express from Edinburgh to London St. Pancras, and one can only say that, judging by the disgraceful state of its bodyside paintwork, something nasty appears to have befallen this machine, perhaps a chronic malfunction of the train heating boiler which sent scalding water cascading down the bodyside.
A.E.R. Cope

Hauling an amazing assortment of freight vehicles of various shapes and sizes, an unidentified BR/Sulzer Type 2 emerges from the southern portal of Blea Moor tunnel, some time in mid-1965. This spot is far from the nearest road, and entails a two miles-long walk along a boggy track, which is certainly not to be undertaken without walking boots or waterproofs. One cannot simply dash back to the car if the weather suddenly changes for the worst, not that such things ever happen on the Settle & Carlisle! Judging by the largely cloudy conditions, the photographer appears to have been fortunate to have the sun shining brightly when the train appeared. A suitable reward for determination and perseverance, some might say! Note the dainty MR distant signal and spoil heaps on Blea Moor indicating the position of the tunnel ventilation shafts.

A.E.R. Cope

This illustration of English Electric Type 4 No. D299 approaching Blea Moor tunnel with a southbound freight train also clearly illustrates the course taken by the railway as it passes through Dentdale. Note the long rows of snow fences, which are just visible above the line on the hillside in the distance. The white-painted stationmaster's house at Dent can also be discerned. The black and white striped device is a banner-repeater signal which gives train crews advance indication of an awkwardly sighted signal, in this case Blea Moor's up distant which is located just beyond the tunnel's southern portal. Banner repeaters were only provided to give prior warning of the position (or aspect) of the next signal and did not have to be obeyed. This picture was taken on 13th July 1971.

Peter Fitton

After threading the dank, dark and cavernous depths of the 2,629 yards-long Blea Moor tunnel, the 9.07am Leeds to Carlisle train bursts out into the breathtaking, winter wonderland of Dentdale on 4th January 1984. The contrast could not be more marked! A most interesting feature of the tunnel portal is the stepped channels down each side of the tunnel mouth, which enable beck and flood water to be contained as it runs off the moor. On reaching track level the water is channelled into underground drains. In this shot the channels are clearly visible, but full of snow! Construction of the tunnel was one of the most difficult and protracted civil engineering feats undertaken by the engineers and navvies building the S&C line. Parts of the tunnel are 500 feet below the moor, and seven shafts were sunk from the surface, work proceeding from sixteen separate faces. It took five years from 1870 to 1875 to excavate the tunnel, which is one of the most outstanding, perhaps *the* most outstanding, engineering achievements on the entire route.

Les Nixon

Pictured on the penultimate day of through freight working on the S&C line, 12th May 1983, an unidentified Class 40 is about to plunge into Blea Moor tunnel with a Carlisle to Healey Mills train. Unfortunately, the dull conditions do little to enhance the magnificent surroundings of Dentdale. In days gone by there was a signal box at Dent Head, but this was closed in April 1965. A landmark in this photograph is Shale cutting, on the extreme left, which is sometimes blocked by snow during the winter.

Author

In the author's opinion, Dentdale is the most beautiful landscape traversed by the S&C line, and in this illustration a diverted Manchester to Glasgow train, hauled by Class 47 No. 47 440, is pictured crossing Dent Head viaduct in April 1989. Photographic spots do not come much better than this! Note that the coaches are in InterCity livery, apart from the blue/grey full brake on the rear. Constructed of blue limestone between 1870 and 1875, Dent Head viaduct is situated in a reasonably sheltered location, compared to others on the line which are totally exposed to the harsh weather conditions prevalent in this area. It is 177 yards long and stands 100 feet above the valley. The central pier is specially strengthened.   *Jim Winkley*

The S&C line sometimes seems to have its own weather patterns, perhaps the fickle nature of the climate being the only consistent characteristic. The high winds and driving, almost horizontal, rain during the winter combine to deter all but the most hardy and determined railway photographer but, occasionally, there can be brilliant spells of winter weather, as seen here. In this memorable picture a pair of unidentified Class 25s, marshalled between two independent snowploughs, are seen in Dentdale on 25th April 1981. The 25s had presumably been clearing snow in the vicinity, possibly in nearby Shale cutting which, as previously stated, is especially vulnerable to blockage. Sunshine and deep snow - what more could a photographer ask for? *Peter Fitton*

Apparently taken from the verandah of Dent Head signal box, this portrait shows BR/Sulzer 2,500hp Type 4 No. D186 powering an up freight on 28th May 1966. By this date the box was out of use, as evidenced by the bare signal post behind the locomotive. A shift spent here on a wild Pennine night, with the wind howling and rain lashing the windows, must have been an unforgettable experience, and maybe a frightening one at times. But during the summer months the box's lofty position, high above Dentdale, offered unbeatable moorland vistas, so the hard life for the signalmen here certainly had its compensations. No. D186 was amongst the final batch of 'Peaks' to enter service, which occurred in November 1962. Withdrawn in December 1982, it was eventually broken-up at Swindon Works almost three years later, in October 1985.

Colour-Rail

A diverted London to Glasgow relief train crosses Arten Gill viaduct behind English Electric Type 4 2,700hp Co-Co No. 424 on 29th July 1972. Few pictures of these machines on the S&C line were submitted for this album, not surprisingly perhaps, as they only worked over the line occasionally on diverted West Coast services when allocated to the LMR from the late 1960s until 1974. Passengers on diverted trains were no doubt frustrated by the extra hours' journey time they were obliged to endure, but on this occasion the weather seemed to be fine and the travellers were hopefully enjoying the unparalleled natural beauty of Dentdale as the train sped along. No. 424 was introduced in June 1968 and was later named *Vanguard* by the Western Region. It was withdrawn from traffic in February 1991 and was scrapped by contractors at Old Oak Common depot seven months later.

Peter Fitton

The steep climb from the road in Dentdale to Arten Gill viaduct has probably left many a railway photographer breathless, and when they reached a photographic spot above the viaduct the view was, one might say, absolutely breathtaking! This masterpiece was taken in superb lighting conditions in the autumn of 1987, and shows a Class 47 rushing across the viaduct with a morning Leeds to Carlisle train; the photographer appears to have been lucky with the sun. Only the distant conifer plantations mar the scene. Arten Gill viaduct, a most graceful eleven-arch structure, was built entirely of stone known as Dent marble, which is dark grey limestone with white fossils. Construction of the 220 yards-long viaduct commenced on 3rd May 1871 and took four years to complete.

Jim Winkley

Judging by the fumes being emitted by the locomotive, the driver of English Electric 2,000hp Type 4 No. D224 *Lucania* has the power full on as it climbs the brief 1 in 264 gradient from Arten Gill to Dent station with a diverted West Coast Main Line express on 2nd October 1966. Note the LMSR-designed coach formed immediately behind the engine: at that time many of these were still in service, and some even survived long enough to be painted in blue/grey livery. This picture was taken from a signal gantry adjacent to Dent signal box, a classic photographic location made famous by the late Bishop Eric Treacy. The backdrop is provided by Wold Fell, beneath which the majestic Arten Gill viaduct is visible. *Neville Simms*

In this, another vintage 1960s picture taken at Dent on the same day as the previous shot, a rather dirty BR/Sulzer 2,500hp 1Co-Co1 locomotive, No. D30, rounds the curve through the station with the southbound 'Thames-Clyde Express'. Note the first coach appears to be carrying roofboards, a feature no longer seen on regular passenger trains. Note also the remains of the snow fences in the field behind the train and the steeply-graded road bridge, beyond the station, which carries the 'coal road' across the railway. This remote road, which crosses the high moorland between Dent and Garsdale stations, was originally built to serve coal pits on the slopes of Widdale Fell. Most unusually for the S&C line, the road bridge was built entirely of brick. Note the tank wagon, in the cattle dock siding, which had presumably suffered a defect and been detached from a freight train.

Neville Simms

The southern portal of Rise Hill tunnel is clearly visible in the distance as Brush Type 4 Co-Co No. 1965 rounds the curve through the deep cutting at the approach to Dent station on 16th July 1972. The train appears to be a diverted West Coast Main Line service. Sadly, even if the rolling stock seen here was still available, it would not be possible to recreate this picture today due to the proliferation of conifer plantations on the moorland surrounding the tunnel and the disappearance of the telegraph poles. No. 1965 was one of a substantial batch of these engines constructed at Crewe Works, from where it emerged in October 1965. Under the TOPS renumbering scheme it became No. 47 265 and later, following the fitting of electric train heating equipment, assumed the identity No. 47 591. In July 1989 it was equipped with long-range fuel tanks and became No. 47 804.

Peter Fitton

Settle and Carlisle weather at its worst! The diverted 9.35am Glasgow to Manchester Red Bank sidings empty newspaper train, hauled by Class 47 No. 47 206, approaches the northern portal of Rise Hill tunnel during a heavy snowstorm in March 1986. This was one of the longest trains seen on the line at this period and was sometimes composed of almost twenty vehicles - a mammoth load. In times gone by, when West Coast Main Line diversions occurred, this train often produced a Class 40, but by this date - apart from the prototype - all of these machines had been withdrawn, so a Class 47 was the best that could be hoped for on this train. On a clear day the view from this spot is breathtaking and trains can be picked out in the distance approaching Garsdale station; it is, however, one of the most rarely photographed locations on the line due to its inaccessibility. *Author*

Photographed against the magnificent snow-covered setting of Garsdale, with Rise Hill dominating the background, Class 47 No. 47 501 heads a Cleethorpes to Carlisle special train on 27th February 1993. The InterCity-liveried carriages, and Class 47 in BR Parcels Sector livery, make an interesting, and certainly extremely colourful, combination. The section between Garsdale station and Rise Hill tunnel is one of the relatively few stretches of level track on the S&C line, and was selected as the location for water troughs.

Les Nixon

In the past the S&C line was always a vital freight link, with passenger traffic revenue being negligible in comparison. In the mid-1970s its role as a freight artery was further reinforced when, as previously mentioned, the West Coast Main Line was modernised and catch points removed. The latter were needed to protect the line in the event of a runaway of an unbraked vehicle. This upgrading resulted in many additional unbraked freight trains being permanently booked to run over the S&C line, many of which were powered by English Electric Type 4s (or Class 40s as they were later known). These locomotives dated from the late 1950s and during their zenith they worked named expresses from London termini, including 'The Royal Scot' and 'The East Anglian'. But by the 1970s they had been replaced on such trains and were largely relegated to secondary passenger and heavy freight work, and became the staple power on S&C line freight traffic. In this everyday scene from the early 1980s, No. 40 125 plods through Garsdale with a Carlisle to Tinsley working on 15th April 1981.

Les Nixon

Top right: In this panoramic view, taken on a typically overcast and misty day in July 1967, an unidentified BR/Sulzer 'Peak' locomotive takes the up 'Thames-Clyde Express' through Garsdale station. The bridge on the extreme left carries the line over the remote 'coal road' to Dent station. Garsdale was the junction for the Hawes branch, being known as 'Hawes Junction' until 1932, and was the only passenger junction station on the S&C line. When the line was built the MR had plans for a railway village of thirty cottages clustered around the station, and a sizeable engine shed. Its plans had to be scaled down for financial reasons, and only sixteen houses were constructed, and a modest locomotive shed, which was mainly used by engines working the branch trains. The isolated and windswept station was the focus of the local community and church services were held in the down platform waiting room, while the water-tank house was adapted for use as the village hall. It was the venue for concerts and dances for many years, until it was demolished in 1971. Perhaps the most famous installation at Garsdale was the turntable, with its protective stockade of old sleepers.   *J. Spencer Gilks*

Bottom right: Photographed against a background of bare moorland, two immaculately turned-out Class 47s, Nos. 47 850 and 47 845, brighten up a rather overcast day as they approach Garsdale with the empty stock of the Royal Train on 3rd May 1991. No doubt two Class 47s were rostered for the train in case of a potentially embarrassing locomotive failure. Apparently HM the Queen, and presumably HRH the Duke of Edinburgh, had left the train at Kirkby Stephen, unfortunately missing the S&C line's most spectacular scenery. No doubt heads would have rolled at the Palace if the Duke discovered what they had missed!
Hugh Ballantyne

GARSDALE TO KIRKBY STEPHEN

The snow-covered slopes of Mossdale Moor, and Widdale Fell beyond, provide a magnificent setting for this portrait of the 9.07am Leeds to Carlisle train at Lunds. Motive power is provided by Class 45 No. 45 142 and this photograph was taken on 3rd March 1984. The road from Sedburgh to Hawes is indicated by the two sets of dry-stone walls, while the course of the Garsdale to Hawes branch line can also be seen. *Hugh Ballantyne*

An unknown Class 47 crosses Lunds viaduct with a diverted West Coast Main Line express on 2nd May 1987, with the distinctive, and on this occasion rather sombre, outline of Wild Boar Fell on the horizon. This viaduct, made entirely of stone, is 103 yards-long and stands 63 feet above ground. The arches each have a span of 45 feet. This is a particularly bleak and exposed section of the S&C line, where the line crosses a watershed from where tributaries flow to the river Ouse, which meets the sea on the east coast, and the river Lune, which enters the sea near Lancaster, on the west coast. In addition, a few miles further on, there is the source of the river Eden which the S&C line follows virtually all of the way to Carlisle. Note the lonely Moorcock to Kirkby Stephen road on the right.   *Author*

Bare moorland stretching as far as the eye can see, the towering mass of Wild Boar Fell, clouds scudding across the sky, the lonely weather-beaten signal box, all combine to produce this memorable Ais Gill scene. The train is the diverted 'Royal Scot' from Glasgow to London hauled by Brush Type 4 No. D1852, and this picture was taken in the mid-1960s. At that time Ais Gill had yet to be 'rationalised' and still boasted up and down loop lines and, of course, all the signals were apparently still operational, thus adding to the attractions of this outstanding location.   *A.E.R. Cope*

Ais Gill summit is probably one of the best known locations on the S&C line, perhaps *the* best known, but strangely very few photographs showing the signal box were submitted for inclusion in this album. This is a pity bearing in mind the box was such a landmark. This scarcity of pictures is probably explained by the fact that the signal box was taken out of use relatively early, in January 1981, and also that photographers preferred the more impressive shot of trains approaching the summit with Wild Boar Fell in the immediate background. Following closure of the box, the area of the summit became rather untidy for a time as a result of the down loop being removed, as seen here in this portrait of a 'Peak' heading northwards on a Nottingham to Glasgow train in the spring of 1982. An interesting feature of the signal box was the walkway from the rear of the building, which gave access to the field at the back.

John Whiteley

The classic Ais Gill scene! Photographed against the towering backdrop of Wild Boar Fell, Brush Type 4 No. 1838, powering a diverted Glasgow to Manchester express, nears the summit after almost fifteen miles of continuous climbing from Ormside. The engine was still painted in two-tone green livery which, in the author's opinion, suited these locomotives much better than the uninspiring rail blue which was in vogue at the time. This picture was taken on 18th July 1971. No. 1838 was built by Brush Traction Ltd. and entered traffic in May 1965.

Peter Fitton

The author well remembers a perfect evening at Ais Gill in July 1979 when an up freight train, double-headed by Class 40s, appeared. To say the least, the locomotives were being driven with a sense of urgency as they pounded up the 1 in 100 towards the summit, the thunderous noise from the locomotives' exhaust reverberating off the fells and totally shattering the silence of an otherwise peaceful, remote spot. The train engine is No. 40 068 but, unfortunately, part of the number of the leading locomotive appears to have been 'washed off', and is unidentifiable. At this time the S&C line was especially busy due to the East Coast Main Line being blocked by a rockfall inside Penmanshiel tunnel, and there was a steady procession of diverted freight workings at Ais Gill during that memorable evening.

Author

Above: Another classic Ais Gill scene, but this time from a much earlier period! The 'Peaks' took over haulage of the S&C line's daytime express services from steam traction in 1961, and were a regular sight on the route for more than a quarter of a century until their demise in 1988. In this illustration No. D18, hauling the down 'Thames-Clyde Express', has just breasted Ais Gill summit and begins the long descent towards Carlisle. No. D18 began life at Derby Works in December 1960 and became No. 45 121 under the TOPS renumbering scheme in February 1974. It remained in service until November 1987 and was, co-incidentally, also scrapped at Derby Works. This picture was taken in August 1966. *Brian Magilton*

Opposite page: This panoramic view from the slopes of Wild Boar Fell towards Mallerstang Common shows clearly the course taken by the railway. The Moorcock to Kirkby Stephen road is in the middle of the shot, while on the right, but mostly hidden by trees, are the infant waters of the river Eden. Note how the railway and road rapidly part company as the road loses height, but the railway remains on a ledge high above the bottom of the valley. A class 40, pulling a lengthy southbound freight, is almost lost in the landscape as it crosses Ais Gill viaduct. The S&C line has been described as the most spectacular route in England, and with fabulous scenery like this who would dare question that description? Some would say it is, without doubt, the most spectacular main line route in Great Britain. A July 1979 picture. *Author*

Photographed on 8th April 1983, Class 25 No. 25 302, in charge of a Mossend yard to Healey Mills freight, crosses Ais Gill viaduct, which is officially known as 'Bridge No. 137'. The four-arch viaduct is 87 yards-long and each of the spans measures 45 feet. The structure stands 75 feet above the floor of the valley. Most of the Class 25s were constructed by BR, but No. 25 302 was an exception, being built by Beyer Peacock, and entering traffic in May 1966 as No. D7652. It lasted until June 1985 and was cut-up at Doncaster Works just over a year later.

Author

The 'alternative' Ais Gill viaduct photographic position! The viaduct carries the S&C line across Ais Gill beck, and many thousands of pictures must have been taken at this outstanding location over the years. This is, however, the first shot the author has seen taken from this angle looking down the side of the fell from above the tracks, and an extremely interesting - and very different - picture has resulted. Class 47 No. 47 439 heads the diverted 8.35am Euston to Inverness across the viaduct on 25th March 1989. *Hugh Ballantyne*

A blizzard at Ais Gill! The S&C line is famous for its rapidly changing weather conditions, when a calm, warm, sunny day can quickly deteriorate. On 8th April 1983 the author enjoyed a lunchtime cup of tea and a sandwich in a cafe at Ais Gill Moor cottages - after an early frost it had been an unbelievably glorious spring morning. But the splendid weather proved deceptive: as the sun disappeared the temperature dropped, and menacing black clouds started to scud across the sky on a stiffening breeze. Later in the afternoon conditions worsened considerably and the transformation was completed when it started to snow, just as the first of the afternoon freights was due. When the train appeared it crossed Ais Gill viaduct in a raging snowstorm that completely hid the fells, which had been dappled by sunshine earlier in the day. Class 46 No. 46 014 is seen crossing the viaduct on that memorable occasion. But, soon afterwards, the weather dramatically changed once again........ *Author*

..... and by the time the 1.10pm Carlisle to Healey Mills freight hove into view the snow had gone and the sun was shining brightly once again! Here, this train is seen climbing steadily past the fells of Mallerstang Common with Class 40 No. 40 063 in command. This locomotive was one of a number originally allocated to Haymarket shed, Edinburgh, when new in March 1960. The Scottish Region fitted these locomotives with slightly non-standard four digit headcode panels and removed some handrails plus the top lamp brackets, thus giving the front end a distinctive appearance.

Author

After the storm! Seen in brilliant, freak lighting conditions as it powers up the 1 in 100 gradient towards Ais Gill, the train depicted in the previous shot is within sight of the summit. Note the parcels van, marshalled immediately behind the engine, which was presumably defective and *en route* for repair. No. 40 063 had exactly one year of active life remaining when this picture was taken, being withdrawn in April 1984. But it remained intact for a further three years, until it was broken-up by Vic Berry Ltd., of Leicester in June 1987. *Author*

A light sprinkling of snow lying on the slopes of Wild Boar Fell forms a picturesque backdrop to this illustration of Class 31 No. 31 404 descending the gradient from Ais Gill towards Birkett tunnel, on a memorable early April morning in 1983. The locomotive's appearance is enhanced by a white bodyside stripe, which really brightens up the engine's otherwise drab and unimaginative rail blue livery. The stripe is believed to have been applied when No. 31 404 was based at Finsbury Park depot, and was used to distinguish locomotives fitted with electric train heating equipment. This would certainly have been needed on the morning of this photograph, which began with severe overnight frost, but the temperature quickly rose when the sun appeared in the almost cloudless sky.   *Author*

The demise of the Class 40s and 'Peaks' in the 1980s, and subsequent replacement of S&C line locomotive-hauled trains by 'Sprinters', were developments that were probably regretted by the majority of enthusiasts. Mercifully the line itself has survived, but the trains that traversed it changed forever, and some would say not for the better. So, in these circumstances, who would have anticipated the appearance of a 'Deltic' in ordinary passenger traffic, albeit on a West Coast diverted train? But on 13th March 1999 this is precisely what happened, and in this marvellous picture No. D9000 *Royal Scots Grey* is seen coasting down from Birkett tunnel towards Kirkby Stephen with a Birmingham to Edinburgh train. One wonders if the passengers appreciated how lucky they were! This machine made its return to the main line in November 1996 and during the following summer was hired by Virgin Trains, undertaking numerous workings on scheduled services. *Les Nixon*

The breathtaking vista from this location, near the northern entrance to Birkett tunnel, is probably one of the most impressive on the S&C line on a clear day, particularly when the tops of the distant Pennine Range are flecked with snow. Needless to say, it is also one of the most photographed! Note the telegraph poles, items of railway furniture which are now rarely seen, and add considerable atmosphere to the shot. Here, Class 31 No. 31 404 is illustrated climbing the 1 in 100 gradient towards the tunnel in early April 1983. This is only a moderately-powered locomotive, but would not have been unduly exerted by the train's lightweight four-coach formation. BR's closure plan for the line, announced later the same year, sparked a massive upsurge of public interest in the route, and a year later the same train - full of people taking their 'last' trip over the line - would have boasted at least a ten-vehicle load, probably hauled by a 'Peak'.

Author

The overwhelming majority of pictures in this album were taken in an orthodox way, from well-known locations with the objective of portraying a train amidst the stunning scenic grandeur of the S&C line. But here is something different! Using considerable imagination and ingenuity the photographer has produced this masterpiece, an unconventional shot of Class 47 No. 47 597 passing Wharton, a tiny hamlet just south of Kirkby Stephen, with a Carlisle to Leeds train on 5th May 1990. It is doubtful if many pictures have been taken from this farm track over the years. Perhaps it could be titled the hill farmer's view of the S&C line!

Les Nixon

Right: Most railway enthusiasts who were around at the time can remember what they were doing on 11th August 1968, the day this picture was taken. That was a melancholy day for many when BR ran its 'last' steam train, from Liverpool to Carlisle and return via the S&C line. This train will always be remembered as the 'Fifteen Guinea Special', due to the exorbitant fare charged to travel on this so-called 'last' train. Brush Type 4 No. D1820, in pleasing two-tone green colours, preceded the special on an unidentified southbound express and is seen here passing Kirkby Stephen, with the Pennines once again visible on the horizon.   *Jim Winkley*

Left: Photographs taken on the S&C line in high summer tend to be affected by haze (or rain, of course, for even more unfortunate souls!) as evidenced in this picture of English Electric Type 4 1Co-Co1 No. D289 running downhill through Kirkby Stephen on 18th July 1971 with a ballast working in tow. Sadly, the fine view along Mallerstang Common usually obtained from this location is almost entirely hidden. Despite the introduction of BR's ghastly corporate blue colour scheme in 1965, many locomotives were at this time still to be seen in the familiar green livery, though many of these had hardly been improved aesthetically by the application of all-over yellow panels on their front ends, as seen here.   *Peter Fitton*

KIRKBY STEPHEN TO APPLEBY

The day this picture was taken, 1st March 1986, was bitterly cold in the fells, and followed an overnight snowfall, which apparently blocked Shale cutting, in Dentdale. The author was a passenger on the morning Carlisle to Leeds train, hauled by Class 47 No. 47 559, and this ran normally as far as Kirkby Stephen (which was still closed at that time). Incredibly, the usually peaceful station area was a hive of activity. There was a Class 37, sandwiched between two snow-covered independent snowploughs, ticking over in the rarely-used cattle dock siding, while a number of staff were apparently examining the snowploughs and locomotive to ensure they were fit to return to Carlisle. Much to the consternation of some travellers, the passenger train was reversed onto the down line and then proceeded to Blea Moor at quite a cautious pace, where the up line was regained. Judging by the build-up of snow in vulnerable cuttings, BR staff had clearly put in considerable effort to reopen the line, and all for just four trains! In this shot No. 37 226 is seen leaving Kirkby Stephen with its snowploughs attached, presumably *en route* to its base at Carlisle. *Peter Walton*

The Settle & Carlisle at its best! Photographed in stunning weather conditions with brilliant lighting, and low clouds scudding across the fells in the distance, the 8.25am Leeds to Carlisle train passes Waitby on 25th November 1989. This lovely scene is enhanced by the train's most interesting motive power, a Class 47 piloted by two Class 20s. For the record the Class 47 is No. 47 444 *University of Nottingham*, while the Class 20s are Nos. 20 061 and 20 093, the occasion being one of the former Provincial Sector's 'unusual motive power' promotions which were designed to attract the enthusiast fraternity to the line's trains during the quieter winter period. The Class 47 returned in charge of the 12.42pm Carlisle to Leeds, but with a different pair of Class 20s, Nos. 20 021 and 20 026. Perhaps one day this enterprising exercise could be repeated with a preserved Class 40 or 'Peak'; it would certainly be wholeheartedly welcomed by many diesel locomotive aficionados. *Hugh Ballantyne*

Right: The photographer must have been disappointed by the gloomy weather conditions at Waitby on 3rd May 1985 as he waited to capture on film the 10.40am Carlisle to Leeds train. But his spirits must have been suddenly lifted as the truly astounding sight of Class 37 No. 37 095 on S&C line passenger duty hove into view around the bend. For reasons unknown to the author these machines rarely venture on to the S&C line, perhaps because few drivers at the depots which normally supply crews for the S&C route are trained on them. *Hugh Ballantyne*

Left: No. 47 444 *University of Nottingham* is seen again, but this time working without assistance. Here it powers the 12.37pm Carlisle to Leeds service across the snowy wastes of Waitby on 25th February 1989. By this time more modern Mk.2 coaches had largely replaced the somewhat decrepit Mk.1 vehicles which had previously been used, a change for the better which would be welcomed by most passengers except, of course, those standard class travellers who preferred the privacy of a compartment! Six months later the cramped and appallingly designed 'Sprinters' were introduced, on which unfortunate passengers can find themselves in a seat without a window. *Hugh Ballantyne*

A shaft of sunshine and sprinkling of snow on the fells combine to produce a gem of a picture of Class 45 No. 45 143, hurrying downhill across Smardale viaduct with the 9.07am from Leeds to Carlisle on 18th January 1984. This picture, which has been published before, is one of the author's favourite S&C line photographs which, in his view, is ample justification for publishing it again! No. 45 143 was named *5th Royal Inniskilling Dragoon Guards* during a ceremony at St. Pancras station on 30th November 1964, but in June 1985 '*1685-1985*' was added to the name to commemorate the regiment's tercentenary. The 'Peak' was presumably renamed at another ceremony, new plates doubtless being cast for this occasion. Despite the distinction of, in effect, carrying two different names, No. 45 143's career was terminated when it was withdrawn in May 1987, and the end eventually came at MC Metal Processing, Glasgow, in March 1994.

Hugh Ballantyne

Another shot at Smardale, this time taken in much more agreeable conditions, showing a pair of Class 50s - Nos. 50 024 *Vanguard* piloting 50 050 *Fearless* - powering the southbound 'Fellsman 2' railtour on 23rd April 1988. These locomotives were (as previously stated) fairly common visitors to the S&C line on West Coast Main Line diverted services up to the mid-1970s. The Class 50s were frequently double-headed, as seen here, but this brave attempt to re-create the past was unfortunately ruined by the colourful, some would say rather garish, Network South-East livery in which the engines, and most of the coaching stock, were painted. In addition, the uniform livery was spoilt by the inclusion of two 'odd' vehicles towards the middle of the train. But at least the Class 50s provided a change from Class 47s!

John Whiteley

Right: An unidentified Class 25 in green livery approaches the former Crosby Garrett station with a short southbound freight in June 1966. The station serving this attractive Pennine village was closed as long ago as 6th October 1952, and the goods yard was also out of commission by the time of this photograph, as evidenced here by the deserted sidings. The signal box was taken out of regular use on 12th April 1965, but remained available for use in emergencies until 1967. Despite the wet and rather gloomy conditions, almost the entire layout of this S&C line wayside station and goods yard is in view. The north ends of the station platforms are just visible in the shot, plus part of a retaining wall. Both platforms were located in a deep cutting and required retaining walls, both of which were substantially built of stone. *J. Spencer Gilks*

Left: The same location as that in the previous illustration is seen again, twenty-five years later: spot the difference! Class 47 No. 47 475 approaches Crosby Garrett with a Leeds-bound service on 22nd October 1990. The site of Crosby Garrett goods yard is now home for a profusion of mature silver birch trees which, at the time of this picture, were a riot of brilliant autumn colours. By the date of this photograph most trains on the S&C line were formed of the dreadful 'Sprinter' units so, perhaps, this locomotive-hauled working was deputising for an unavailable 'Sprinter'. *Les Nixon*

Photographed in dramatic, freak lighting conditions, for which the S&C line is justly famed, a four-car d.m.u. approaches Crosby Garrett with a southbound service on 29th March 1986. The Pennine fells are almost completely concealed by a huge mass of threatening black storm clouds. The train is presumably a 'Dales Rail' working, which ran from the Leeds area on selected weekends for the benefit of ramblers. The Yorkshire Dales National Park Authority initiated these services in 1975, and served remote stations which had been closed by BR in May 1970. Fortunately, most of these stations had remained untouched by BR's demolition experts since closure and were in good condition, apart from the down platform at Ribblehead which had been removed. In July 1986 some intermediate stations were reopened on a regular basis and the 'Dales Rail' trains were no longer needed. Amazingly, while many individuals and organisations served by the route were making strenuous efforts to promote the S&C line in a variety of ways, BR was still proceeding with its closure proposal as if it was totally detached from reality. *Les Nixon*

A stranger on the Settle & Carlisle! Scottish-based Class 26 No. 26 031 is pictured at Griseburn on 21st May 1989 in charge of a short Civil Engineer's Department working. This distinctive locomotive was built by the Birmingham Railway Carriage & Wagon Company as No. D5331 and entered traffic in June 1959. It only survived in service for a further five months after this portrait was taken and was cut-up at MC Metal Processing, Glasgow, in September 1990. There was a quarry at Griseburn, situated on the down side, which was served by a number of sidings, the signal box being officially known as 'Griseburn Ballast Sidings'. It is not known precisely when quarrying ceased, but connections to the sidings were removed in 1971, and the signal box was closed in January 1981.

Peter Walton

Class 40 No. 40 139 growls up the bank past Breaks Hall with a lengthy afternoon freight from Carlisle on 5th June 1981. The southern portal of the 571 yards-long Helm tunnel is partially visible in the background while, once again, the outline of the Pennine Range forms a distant backdrop. At this point the railway has been climbing steadily at 1 in 100 for two miles and this gradient continues, with minor variations, for a further thirteen miles until Ais Gill summit is reached. No. 40 139 emerged from Vulcan Foundry in April 1961 as No. D339 and, despite its smart appearance in this illustration, was destined to last in service for only a further eight months after this shot was taken.

Chris Evans

Class 40 No. 40 122, alias D200, enhances this magnificent, panoramic landscape shot as it climbs towards Helm tunnel with the morning train from Carlisle to Leeds on 7th September 1983. The load of four coaches was hardly likely to strain No. D200 unduly, despite the long climb ahead to Ais Gill summit. Unfortunately, the distant mountains are slightly obscured by haze, a common occurrence in this part of the world. In the author's experience visibility on the S&C line is always clearest following rain.

Les Nixon

Above: On a beautiful morning in September 1983, Class 45 No. 45 055 *Royal Corps of Transport*, which is in quite presentable external condition, makes a quick exit from Helm tunnel with the morning Leeds to Carlisle service. No. 45 055 was built at BR's Crewe Works in December 1960 as No. D84 and was named in June 1966. The removal of its name in March 1985 was obviously a bad omen; it was condemned during the following month! No. 45 055 was scrapped at Vic Berry's Leicester establishment in October 1986.

Author

Opposite page: BR/Sulzer Class 46 No. 46 014 is seen beginning the long climb from Ormside viaduct to Ais Gill with a Carlisle to Healey Mills freight on 3rd June 1981. The vehicle marshalled immediately behind the locomotive is a BR Standard Full Brake, or 'BG' in railwaymen's parlance. The conical-shaped hill in the middle of the picture is Dufton Pike, while the 2,930 feet-high Cross Fell is prominent on the horizon. There was a station at Ormside, serving a tiny rural community, but it was closed from 2nd June 1952.

Chris Evans

A true Christmas card scene! Fresh overnight snow on the branches of lineside trees provides an appealing background as Class 47 No. 47 535 *University of Leicester* makes a speedy departure from Appleby with the 10.40am Carlisle to Leeds train on 12th January 1987. Built at Crewe Works as No. D1649 in January 1965, it was allocated No. 47 065 under the TOPS computerised renumbering scheme, but the locomotive was being equipped with electric train heating at the time and emerged from shops as No. 47 535, as seen here.

Peter Walton

APPLEBY TO CARLISLE

Right: An unidentified northbound working enters Appleby station some time during the summer of 1968. The seven-coach train appears to be formed entirely of Metropolitan Cammell d.m.u. vehicles. At this time the few regular passenger workings over the line were either long-distance locomotive-hauled services or Hellifield to Carlisle stopping trains, usually formed of a two-car d.m.u., so perhaps this was a special, maybe originating in the West Riding where units of this type were common. Note how different Appleby station and its environs looked in those days. The goods yard was still in business and Appleby West signal box (just visible behind the tall signal, on the left) still controlled movements at the southern end of the station. In addition, the water tank, water crane (at the end of the up platform) and up siding remained in position. The station itself retained the name 'Appleby West', by which it had been known since 1952, but apparently it officially reverted to simply 'Appleby' in about May 1968. Note the gas lighting and regional colours used for signs and other station fittings, both features that have long since been consigned to history. *Cliff Woodhead*

Left: Flaming June on the Settle & Carlisle! Viewed from the footbridge, the windscreen wipers on Class 25 No. 25 224 appear to be working overtime as it pulls into a very wet Appleby station with the 8.57am Leeds to Carlisle train on 26th June 1982. Note the steam heating boiler is also working hard judging by the amount of steam escaping at the rear of the train. Passengers on the rain-soaked platform appear to be well protected from the elements and the smoking chimney indicates that the station staff have lit a coal fire. Spot the difference - apart from the deterioration in the weather (!) - between this and the previous picture. The station building has, mercifully, survived unscathed, but other structures, such as the water tank, signal box (which was closed in October 1973) and up siding have all been swept away. Perhaps worst of all is the replacement of the ornate gas lamp standards with modern fluorescent lighting, which hardly enhances the station's delightful Victorian atmosphere. Surely, with a little ingenuity, the gas lamps could have been adapted? *Chris Evans*

At night-time the railway takes on an indefinable magic, even at a modestly sized station such as Appleby. The special appeal of the railway after dark is considerably enhanced in this shot by Class 40 No. 40 118, which is seen pausing with the evening Leeds to Carlisle train on 29th December 1984. The example seen here was one of a small batch of Class 40s built by Robert Stephenson & Hawthorns Ltd, at Darlington, this particular locomotive being outshopped in February 1961. Curiously, No. 40 118 featured in a film about the Great Train Robbery, but the choice of this locomotive was most strange, because the engine actually involved, No. D326, was equipped with split indicators! No. 40 118 had another claim to fame due to its long periods out of use at Crewe Works but, even so, it lasted until the very end of the class (apart from No. 40 122) in January 1985 and was the final RSH locomotive in traffic.

Peter Walton

Top right: Careful use of a telephoto lens has produced this unconventional illustration of BR/Sulzer Type 2 No. D5234 crossing Long Marton viaduct with a down freight train on 8th November 1967. Constructed at Derby Works in December 1963, it became No. 25 084 under the TOPS renumbering scheme in February 1974. It was withdrawn from traffic in December 1983 and was scrapped at Swindon Works in June 1986. Long Marton viaduct was built between 1871 and 1874 from stone quarried nearby at Dufton Gill, although brick was also used. It is 108 yards long, 60 feet high and consists of five spans varying in length between 43 and 45 feet. *Neville Simms*

Bottom right: Cars, automatic lifting barriers, a row of houses and a Class 37 on a train of hopper wagons are not immediately identified with the S&C line which is, of course, much more famous for its desolate moorland scenery and lofty viaducts. This, almost urban scene, which is quite different in character to many of the pictures in this album, was taken at Culgaith on 23rd June 1982 and shows No. 37 094 disturbing the peace of the village as it growls through the former station with a train apparently bound for McGhie's siding at Kirkby Thore. The signal box at Culgaith dates from October 1908, while the lifting barriers replaced crossing gates in 1976. The roof of the former station building is visible above the locomotive. *Chris Evans*

The section of the S&C line between Appleby and Carlisle is generally considered by photographers to be somewhat uninspiring compared to the superb moorland stretches elsewhere on the line. Perhaps it is an unfair comparison, after all the stretch south of Kirkby Stephen is really outstanding! Some worthwhile photographic locations are to be found, however, one of the best being this spot above Culgaith tunnel. Here Class 40 No. 40 086 is depicted approaching the tunnel with the afternoon Leeds to Carlisle train in September 1983. The signal box, which controls one of only two level crossings on the line, and remains of the station are visible in the middle of picture. The conical-shaped hill prominent on the horizon is Dufton Pike. It was quite a cloudy evening but, for once, the sun deigned to shine at the crucial moment.   *Author*

Another attractive location north of Appleby is at Eden Lacy, where the railway crosses the river Eden on a 137 yards-long, seven-arch viaduct. This structure, which is clearly visible on the right, was built of local red sandstone between 1871 and 1875. Another point of interest is the collection of buildings, the tops of which are discernible on the extreme left, marking the site of the former Long Meg sidings. These served a mine, from which the mineral anhydrite was extracted, and in the dying days of steam traction on the S&C line the very heavy Long Meg to Widnes (Lancashire) mineral trains were one of the star turns on the route. On one occasion a particularly 'clapped out' steam locomotive took more than 50 minutes to move its train from Kirkby Stephen to Ais Gill, including at least one stop for a blow-up. Unfortunately, the mine, which had been a considerable source of traffic for BR, was closed in the mid-1970s and the complex of sidings fell into disuse. In this picture Class 47 No. 47 453 is heading the 3.55pm Leeds to Carlisle train on 6th July 1985.

Bob Leslie

In this view from the early 1980s, a Glasgow to Nottingham express is seen passing the former station at Lazonby, the neat stone buildings of which are visible in the background. The identity of the Class 45 locomotive hauling the train is unknown. The photographer is standing above the 99 yards-long Lazonby tunnel; what a pity that the interesting vista is spoilt by a construction site! Originally a cutting was planned at this spot, but the MR changed its mind and a tunnel was built instead in 1871/72. The imposing structure to the right of the up platform is the stationmaster's house. In days gone by there was a signal box at Lazonby controlling movements into the goods yard, which was very busy with livestock traffic. Goods facilities were withdrawn in November 1964 and the signal box was taken out of use in June 1969.

Les Nixon

Pictured on the beautiful afternoon of 2nd May 1987, Class 45 No. 45 124 winds the diverted 9.45am Euston to Glasgow train around the curve at Baron Wood, with the Pennine Range forming a splendid, distant backdrop. Class 45s were probably becoming rare at Carlisle by this date, so the sight of one hauling a long train of air-conditioned InterCity stock was no doubt especially unusual. Presumably the engine was manned by a Carlisle-based driver, who was much more likely to the passed-out to drive 'Peaks' that one based at Preston. No. 45 124 first saw the light of day as No. D28 at Derby in May 1961 and remained in service until January 1988. It met its end at MC Metals Processing's Glasgow works in February 1992.

John Whiteley

Another picture taken in the picturesque Baron Wood area, this time showing Class 40 No. 40 028 (formerly *Samaria*) heading south with the diverted Glasgow to Manchester, Red Bank sidings, empty newspaper train. This scene was recorded on Sunday 29th April 1984. Armathwaite tunnel is visible in the distance. Unlikely though it may seem today, there used to be sidings at Baron Wood which were installed for the use of a landowner who had extensive forestry interests in the area. During the First World War pit props were prepared at the local sawmill and moved by train from Baron Wood sidings. The sidings were closed in 1951 and the main line connection was subsequently removed.

Bob Leslie

Pictured in ideal soft evening lighting conditions, Class 40 No. 40 086 crosses Dry Beck viaduct with the 4.00pm Leeds to Carlisle train on 21st September 1983. This 139 yards-long structure, which is composed of seven 44 feet-long spans, takes the railway across a dell which is normally dry - hence its name. The viaduct was built between 1871 and 1875. Remarkable though it may seem, the train is climbing at 1 in 132, this being the ruling gradient from a point about a mile north of Armathwaite station to just beyond Low House crossing. This is one of the few sections north of Ais Gill where the gradient is against northbound trains.

Bob Leslie

Low House crossing is one of only two level crossings on the S&C line. It takes the minor road from Wetheral to Armathwaite across the railway. The historical records are somewhat vague, but it seems that the signal box dates from October 1890. Lifting barriers replaced the original crossing gates in 1975. The road crosses the tracks on the skew, but a separate foot crossing was provided which crossed the lines at right angles. There is no sign of it in this study, so presumably it had been removed by the date of this photograph, perhaps when the barriers were installed. Here, Class 31 No. 31 410 negotiates the crossing with the 4.35pm Carlisle to Leeds train on 4th June 1983. Note the local bus waiting at the barriers. By this date there were only two daily S&C line passenger trains each way, and doubtless the bus service to Armathwaite was infrequent, to say the least, so this seems to have been a particularly lucky shot.

Bob Leslie

Ancient and ...... well, not so ancient! When this shot of No. D200 working the 4.00pm Leeds to Carlisle train was taken, on 26th August 1983, it was over 25 years old, so can hardly be described as 'modern'. At the time of this picture, the veteran Class 40 had only been working regularly over the S&C line for a few weeks following its refurbishment, hence its absolutely pristine condition in this shot. The signal box at this location was originally on the up side, being moved in 1916 to the position seen here. The siding served Howe & Company's alabaster works which was taken over by another firm in the 1920s, but the original name still survived on the signal box decades later.

Bob Leslie

Top left: The S&C line's sinuous exit from Carlisle past a scrapyard is hardly impressive or inspiring, and a stranger could be forgiven for thinking that the single track led to a factory complex or dock branch. How deceptive! In this view a pair of smartly turned-out Class 31s, Nos. 31 442 and 31 441, take the 4.35pm Carlisle to Leeds train down the sharp, curving gradient out of Carlisle. In the background a trio of Class 25s are lined up awaiting their next duties just south of the signal box, which is partially visible. The station roof can also be seen, in the middle background, on the right. *Bob Leslie*

Bottom left: One of the saddest events for diesel enthusiasts during the 1980s was the withdrawal *en masse* of all the surviving Class 40s in January 1985, the only exception being No. D200 (alias 40 122). They were really very much a 'steam age' diesel, being first introduced on the Liverpool Street to Norwich expresses in March 1958, so this successful and much-loved class really stood the all-important test of time. No. 40 122 had been officially condemned in August 1981, but in early 1983 BR had a flash of inspiration and made the enlightened decision to reinstate the locomotive in green livery. Its return to revenue stock occurred on 24th April 1983. Toton depot was selected to undertake a power unit change, overhaul the bogies and certain electrical components plus, of course, a full repaint. The latter even included white tyres, such was the enthusiasm of the depot's staff. It returned to service in August 1983, working the morning Carlisle to Leeds train and afternoon return working. Here No. D200 is seen posing at the north end of Carlisle station on 28th March 1985, by which time it was the sole survivor of its class. Perhaps the current operator of S&C line services could be persuaded to reintroduce limited diesel-hauled services during the summer months, using preserved traction. Such an enterprising move would undoubtedly be extremely popular and profitable!   *Peter Walton*